WHAT'S BENEATH

PEEKING
UNDERGROUND

by Karen Latchana Kenney

illustrated by Steven Wood

raintree

a Capstone company — publishers for children

Take a look around the park.
What do you see?
People walk and play.
Animals crawl, hop and jump.
Plants stretch towards the sun.

Life is busy ABOVE ground.
What happens BELOW?
Turn the page to peek beneath ...

Beneath the Earth's surface lie layers of soil. Each layer, or horizon, is made of different things. Humus and topsoil are at the top. They have pockets of life and air. Subsoil and loose rock lie further down. They hold rocks, minerals and clay. The deepest horizon is solid rock.

A horizon (topsoil)

O horizon (humus)

The horizons formed over millions of years. Wind and sun beat down on the Earth's surface. Water flowed, froze and flowed again. Rocks, plants and animal remains broke down into smaller and smaller pieces. The new soil settled into layers.

C horizon (loose rock)

R horizon (bedrock)

B horizon (subsoil)

Right on top

Humus is the dark, moist top layer of soil. It's made from dead plants and animals. The remains break down into nutrients. Humus is crumbly and light. Air and water pass easily through it.

mushroom

earthworm

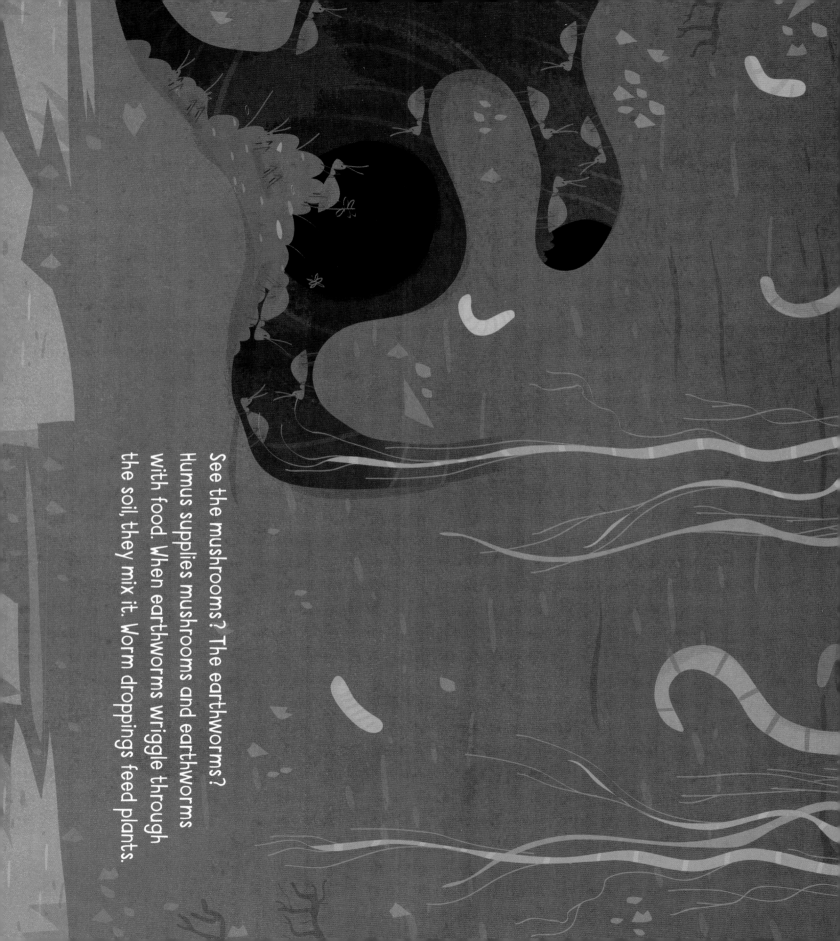

See the mushrooms? The earthworms?
Humus supplies mushrooms and earthworms
with food. When earthworms wriggle through
the soil, they mix it. Worm droppings feed plants.

Buzzing with life

Topsoil is a mix of many things. It includes sand, silt and clay. It also has bits of humus in it. Many tiny creatures live in topsoil. Centipedes, ants and other insects crawl through the soil. Spiders dig holes. Snails and slugs slip and slide.

mole

2

DID YOU KNOW?
Many kinds of bacteria live in topsoil. You can't see them with the naked eye. They're too tiny. Just 5 millilitres (1 teaspoon) of soil can hold close to 1 billion bacteria!

badger

rabbit

fox

Larger animals make burrows in the topsoil. Moles dig tunnels. So do rabbits and badgers. Foxes sometimes live underground too.

Plant roots

What else lives in topsoil? Plant and tree roots! Look just below the stems on this page. See the carrots? Carrots are long, thick roots called taproots. Smaller roots branch off from them.

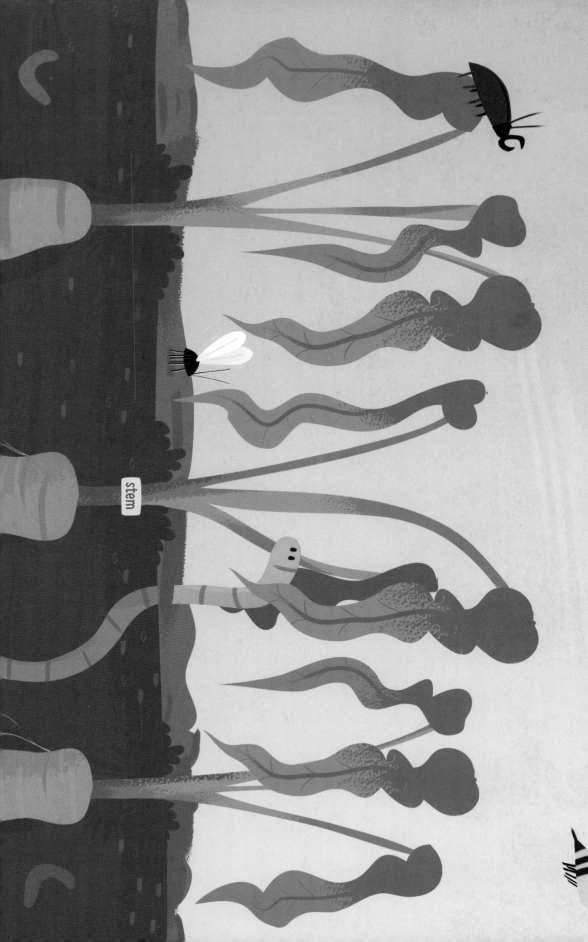

stem

Roots keep plants firmly in the ground.
They take in water and food from the topsoil.
Plants need these things to grow.

taproot

Changing colour

Dig deeper and you'll find subsoil. See the change in colour? The thick subsoil layer is much lighter than topsoil. It may be grey, light brown or even red. Subsoil is made of fine rock and clay. It has tiny amounts of metal in it.

topsoil

subsoil

Water trickles through the layer.
It carries bits of the topsoil above.
But there is little life in subsoil.

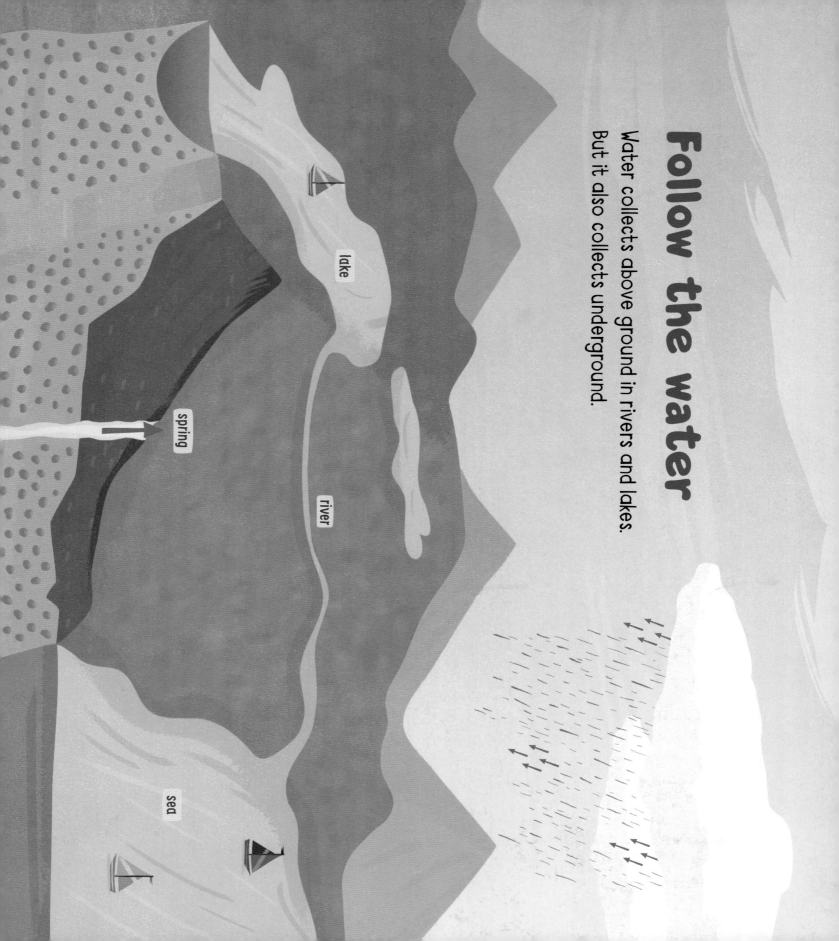

Follow the water

Water collects above ground in rivers and lakes.
But it also collects underground.

lake

spring

river

sea

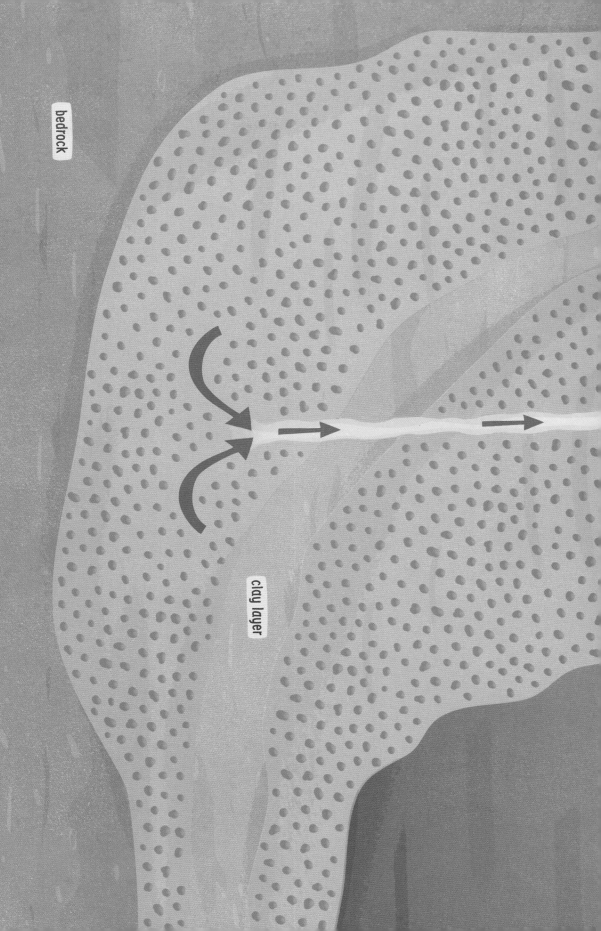

Water is always moving underground. Rain falls from the sky. It seeps into the soil. Gravity pulls it downwards. Rock takes out much of the bacteria and dirt from the moving water. The water collects in a layer of rock. Some water leaves the rock layer through a spring.

bedrock

clay layer

Simply rock

Rock, rock and more rock! Loose, broken rocks mix with soil just below the subsoil. This layer has minerals such as quartz and mica in it. It rests on top of solid rock. Bedrock is a very deep layer. It sits at the bottom edge of the Earth's crust.

loose rock

bedrock

subsoil

Bedrock can be many thousands of metres thick. It's often 10 to 100 times thicker than the loose rock layer above it.

Fossil fuels

Deep inside the bedrock
layer lie fossil fuels.
Oil and natural gas are
fossil fuels. So is coal.

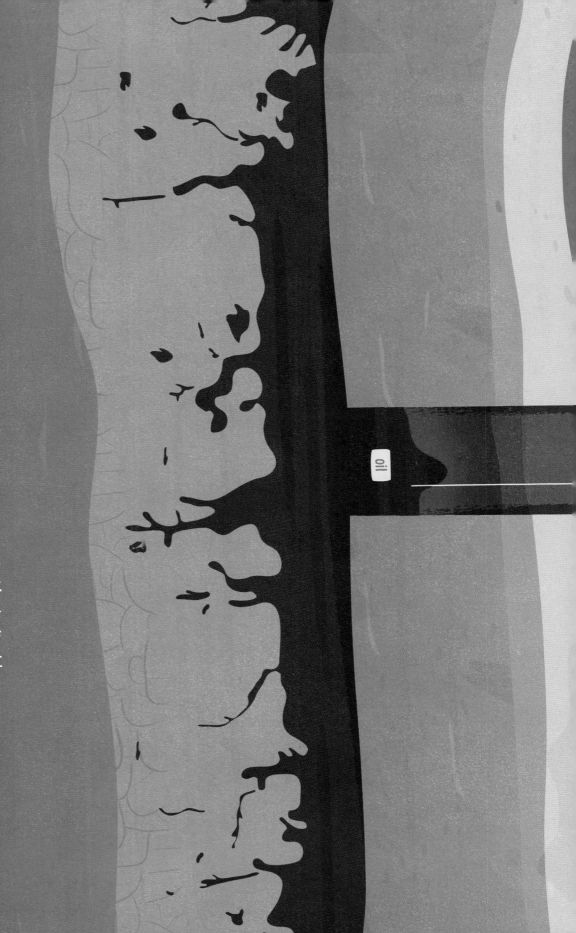

Fossil fuels formed from plants and animals that died long ago. Sand and mud covered the remains over millions of years. The remains sank deeper and deeper into the earth. The weight of the soil and rock on top of them pushed down hard. The pressure and heat turned the remains into fossil fuels.

On the move

Earth's crust is not one piece. It is made of seven major plates. See where the two plates below meet? That line is called a fault line.

Ocean crust is heavy. It slides under the land's crust. The two crusts rub together. Sometimes they get stuck. Earthquakes happen when the crusts break free of each other.

oceanic plate

fault line

volcano

continental plate

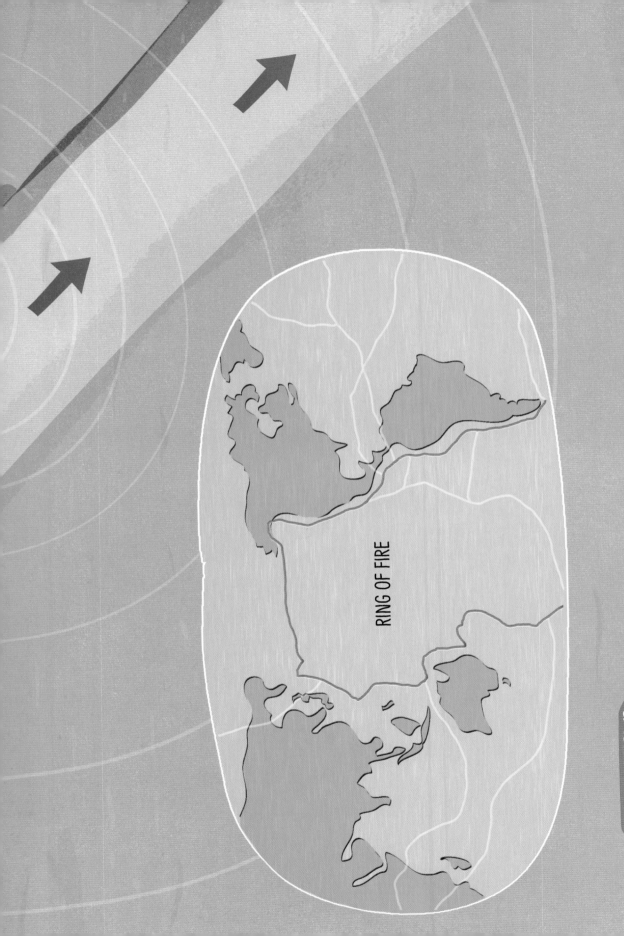

RING OF FIRE

Many large earthquakes happen in the Ring of Fire. This area stretches along the Pacific Ocean. It's at the edge of the Pacific plate. Many volcanoes also line this plate.

Volcano blast

What a sight! It's a volcano!

ash

lava

vent

side vent

Take a look inside. See the vent?
It is a crack in the Earth's crust.
Side vents branch off it. Hot, gooey
molten rock called magma is pushed
up the vents. The volcano erupts!
Lava shoots out. Some cools in the
air and becomes ash.

magma

Below the crust

How far down can we go? The mantle is just below the Earth's crust. It is the Earth's thickest layer. The mantle is 2,900 kilometres (1,800 miles) thick. It is made up of solid and molten rock.

crust

mantle

To the core

Welcome to the centre of our planet! See the outer core and the inner core? The outer core is mostly liquid metal. It is 2,250 km (1,400 miles) thick. Movement inside the outer core makes the Earth a giant magnet. The Earth's poles are on opposite sides of the magnet.

The inner core looks like a ball. It's the hottest part of our planet. It is 1,200 km (750 miles) thick.

NORTH POLE

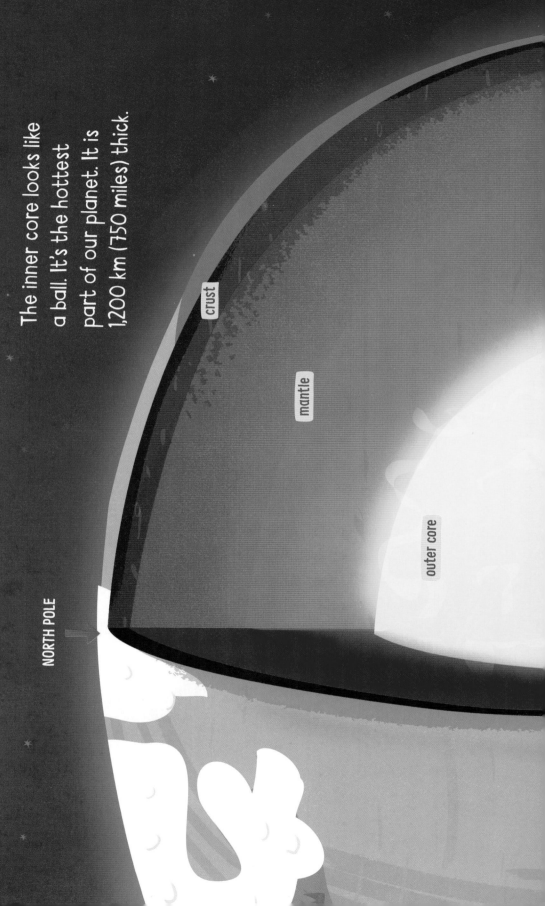

crust

mantle

outer core

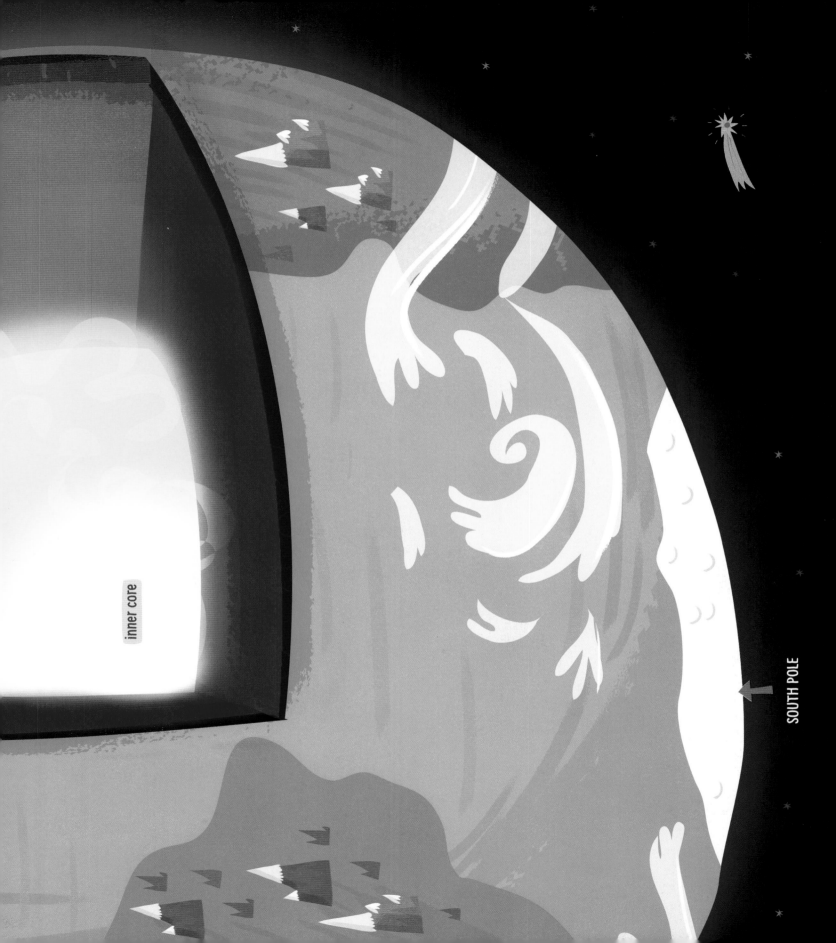

inner core

SOUTH POLE

Back above ground, bees buzz. Squirrels scurry into the trees. Birds pull earthworms from the soil. The grass tickles your toes. Earth is an amazing place, above the surface or underground!

GLOSSARY

bacteria very small living things that exist everywhere in nature

bedrock layer of solid rock beneath the layers of soil and loose gravel

continental having to do with the Earth's land masses

fossil fuel natural fuel formed from the remains of plants and animals; coal, oil and natural gas are fossil fuels

gravity invisible force that pulls objects towards the Earth's core

humus wet, dark part of soil that is made of rotted plants and animals

lava hot, liquid rock that pours out of a volcano when it erupts

magma molten rock found deep inside the Earth

magnet piece of metal that attracts iron or steel; a magnet has two ends called poles

mantle thick layer of hot rock between the Earth's crust and core

mineral solid found in nature that has a crystal structure

molten melted by heat

nutrient part of food, such as a vitamin, that is used for growth

oceanic having to do with the ocean

pressure force made by pressing on something

silt small grains that are smaller than sand and larger than clay; silt is made up of tiny bits of rock

spring source of water that comes from the ground

subsoil layer of the Earth between topsoil and loose rock

taproot the main root of certain plants, such as a carrot

topsoil top layer of soil that is rich with humus

FIND OUT MORE

BOOKS

Experiments with Soil (My Science Investigations), Christine Taylor-Butler (Raintree, 2011)

Rocks and Soil (Moving Up with Science), Peter Riley (Franklin Watts, 2015)

Volcanoes (Learning About Landforms), Chris Oxlade (Raintree, 2014)

WEBSITES

www.bbc.co.uk/bitesize/ks2/science/materials/rocks_soils/read/1/

This site has information, games and a quiz about rocks and soils.

www.ngkids.co.uk/science-and-nature/structure-of-the-earth

Visit this site to find out more about the structure of the Earth.

COMPREHENSION QUESTIONS

1. Why do plants and animals live in the humus and topsoil layers?

2. Explain how fossil fuels form.

3. Why do you think it's so difficult to explore beneath the Earth's crust?

Raintree is an imprint of Capstone Global Library Limited, a company incorporated in England and Wales having its registered office at 264 Banbury Road, Oxford, OX2 7DY – Registered company number: 6695582

www.raintree.co.uk
myorders@raintree.co.uk

Text © Capstone Global Library Limited 2016
The moral rights of the proprietor have been asserted.

ISBN 978 1 4747 6470 4 (paperback)
23 22 21 20 19
10 9 8 7 6 5 4 3 2

British Library Cataloguing in Publication Data
A full catalogue record for this book is available from the British Library.

Editorial Credits
Jill Kalz, editor; Russell Griesmer, designer; Nathan Gassman, creative director; Katy LaVigne, production specialist

Acknowledgements
We would like to thank Bryce Hoppie, PhD, PG, Professor of Geology, Minnesota State University, Mankato, USA, for his invaluable help in the preparation of this book.

Every effort has been made to contact copyright holders of material reproduced in this book. Any omissions will be rectified in subsequent printings if notice is given to the publisher.

All the Internet addresses (URLs) given in this book were valid at the time of going to press. However, due to the dynamic nature of the Internet, some addresses may have changed, or sites may have changed or ceased to exist since publication. While the author and publisher regret any inconvenience this may cause readers, no responsibility for any such changes can be accepted by either the author or the publisher.

Printed and bound in India.

LOOK FOR ALL THE BOOKS IN THE SERIES:

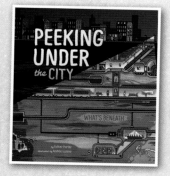